JERRY COKER has played and recorded with
Woody Herman, Stan Kenton, Frank Sinatra, Tony Bennett,
Mel Torme, and other well-known performers.
Mr. Coker has also taught at several universities,
including Indiana University, the University of Miami,
and currently Duke University. He is the author of the
widely acclaimed *Improvising Jazz* (Prentice-Hall).

THE
JAZZ
IDIOM

JERRY COKER

A SPECTRUM BOOK

PRENTICE-HALL, INC. Englewood Cliffs, New Jersey

Library of Congress Cataloging in Publication Data

COKER, JERRY.
  The jazz idiom.

  1. Jazz music.   2. Improvisation (Music)
3. Arrangement (Music)   I. Title.
MT68.C642   781.5'7   75-19250
ISBN 0-13-509851-3
ISBN 0-13-509844-0 pbk.

A SPECTRUM BOOK

10 9 8 7 6 5 4 3 2 1

Printed in the United States of America

PRENTICE-HALL INTERNATIONAL, INC. *(London)*
PRENTICE-HALL OF AUSTRALIA PTY. LTD. *(Sydney)*
PRENTICE-HALL OF CANADA, LTD. *(Toronto)*
PRENTICE-HALL OF INDIA PRIVATE LIMITED *(New Delhi)*
PRENTICE-HALL OF JAPAN, INC. *(Tokyo)*
PRENTICE-HALL OF SOUTHEAST ASIA (PTE.) LTD. *(Singapore)*

*This book is dedicated lovingly to my father, Curtis Coker,
whose encouragement by example inspired me
to devote my life's energies to jazz music*

CONTENTS

PREFACE

There was a time when I'd have protested vehemently the inclusion of many kinds of nonclassical, folk, and popular music under the very general heading of *Jazz*. A jazz band that played an arrangement that did not incorporate improvisation and/or rhythmic swing also offended me if the performance was labeled *Jazz*. In my own way, I suppose I was right, but the overall musical concept was narrow. Jazz has always had its arms outstretched to other domestic and foreign musical styles—even passing styles—and each has enriched the sound of jazz. A "pure" concept would only have restricted the growth of jazz. I like to think of jazz as an "open" style. A pure concept often leads to a "closed" style. This has been demonstrated in history a number of times in musical styles such as, quite recently, ragtime and Dixieland, and perhaps in the not-too-distant future, it will be demonstrated in classical music. Each took a pure course, severing input lines and defending its purity until it became what I would refer to as a "glass-case art," like a museumpiece being protected from change, basking in its perfection. In no way do I mean to denigrate these closed styles, as each has its own greatness and beauty, and a few artistic and canny curators are protecting us against the loss of those styles. But most young players want to be part of a musical world that is actively open, stylistically responding to an ever-changing environment. This attitude also tends to solve the player's economic needs, coincidentally keeping him attuned to current professional needs.

I have grown to realize, too, that in educational circles, jazz and other nonclassical styles such as rock, pop, folk, country and Western have much in common. They are somewhat universally unwelcome—actively or passively—in the university. Each of the styles requires a similar kind of training, including items like studying popular songs, song writing, arranging, improvisation, personal and creative singing styles, keyboard work, modern harmony, electronic instruments, drum set, and even recording techniques, and preparation for teaching the music to another generation. Yet little of the foregoing exists in the present average university curriculum.

To help close this unfortunate gap was my aim in preparing the study outlines contained in this book. The book has been labeled a book for *jazz* study, and indeed it does focus more on jazz than any other nonclassical style, but I welcome students of other styles, knowing that our commonness is much greater than our disparity, and acknowledging that my concept of the word "jazz" has been considerably widened in recent years.

I have observed that students of music often prefer to gain many of their musical tools through self-study, so as to be free to move at their own pace. But almost as often, they lack a blueprint for the activities that would help them achieve their goals. This is why I have chosen an outline form for the book. An outline more readily permits the student to see the direction of his study at all times. In such a condensed form, he can virtually memorize his blueprint and tailor it to suit his individual and stylistic needs. And while it is true that the brevity of an outline does not permit the inclusion of *all* information about the subjects, the outline does make possible the inclusion of many of the most relevant areas of study; each area will recommend sources of information that will lead to an expanded knowledge of the area.

The order of the chapters indicates the approximate sequence of topics as they should be arranged for the most complete understanding of all the topics contained in the book. However, they are not interdependent and can be taken up in any order that answers the student's current areas of interest.

A few last words—**very important ones**—those of you who are not blessed with a rapacious appetite for practice, or whose practice habits are erratic, should turn immediately to the Afterword on page 81.

1

JAZZ HISTORY

Many books have been written on jazz history, but very few of them are suitable for study purposes. A large number of the books were authored by people who were not jazz musicians or even musicians. Even the fundamental definitions given to the lay reader are apt to be more accurate if they are written by someone who practices the craft. Even the musically educated person can miss the point, especially the feeling, in his explanations of jazz, if he is not himself a jazz musician. To compound the problem, very few jazz musicians have made good authors. If our understanding of jazz history is to be more complete and accurate, then the definitions, explanations, and especially the descriptions of individual artists must be written by someone who is a part of jazz. I won't discuss the many books that are personal biographies or autobiographies, nor books that are collections of anecdotes and road stories. Such books are of minimal importance to one who wishes to know about the *music,* and are probably of more value to sociologists than to learning musicians.

A second problem with books on jazz history (and on

music history of any sort) is that although they may serve the masses very well, those who are seriously studying music to become *musicians* rather than music buffs are likely to receive very little information of real musical value. The depth of technical detail required by a serious student would leave the lay leader somewhere along the trail.

Finally, the *real* history of jazz is not contained in words from a book, but in the sounds themselves, which are also rather difficult to obtain. Many recordings are out of print—even the ones of the past decade, let alone those from 1918 to 1965. Most of what *is* available must be researched in catalogs and ordered with fingers crossed. Many historical jazz record collections have been released, but all too often they are neither complete nor accurate. The most complete and accurate collection is *The Smithsonian Collection of Classic Jazz*, which includes a pamphlet of excellent annotations by Martin Williams, who also selected the recordings.[1]

Despite all the problems of researching jazz history, this type of study is of great importance to the student of jazz. It could result in a personal style that has greater depth and a more authoritative voice. Early recordings may have imperfections, both in the music and its reproduction, but each generation has its geniuses and much can be learned from them. Clare Fischer (jazz pianist-composer) was judging a college jazz festival in 1965 when a tenor saxophonist came to him and asked for some critical advice. Clare volunteered that there had been a notable lack of stylistic depth in his playing and suggested that he spend a little more time researching more traditional players. With that the student drew back and exclaimed, "Traditional? Why, my listening

[1] Washington, D.C.: Smithsonian Institute, 1973.

goes all the way back to John Coltrane!" This would give him a grand total of about eight years of "traditional" listening! I was very lucky, because my father was also a jazz musician (an improviser, too). Our home resounded with the great solos of the day, like Coleman Hawkins' "Body and Soul," Jack Jenny's "Stardust," Bunny Berigan's "I Can't Get Started," Benny Goodman's "Sing, Sing, Sing," Art Tatum's "Yesterdays," and many of the best recordings of Duke Ellington, Lester Young, Chuck Berry, John Kirby, etc. When I visited my grandfather, an invasion of the old Victrola would result in the discovery of people like Paul Whiteman, Isham Jones, Bix Beiderbecke, and other, even earlier players. Many of their solos were firmly fixed in my memory long before I began playing. Almost as important, I became aware of the reactions of *musicians* to the music even before I could understand exactly what they were saying.

My upbringing was pretty unique. By the time I picked up an instrument, I'd heard a lifetime of jazz music on records, plus hearing my father improvise often in practice, in jam sessions, at rehearsals, and in performance. I *knew* what I wanted to play, in terms of content, from hearing the best of jazz repeatedly. I cannot always say the same of my improvisation students (unless we've instigated a strenuous program of listening). Hence they are sometimes restricted in their choices of what to play largely because they haven't heard enough of the music. And that's why jazz history should probably precede most other jazz endeavors, especially improvisation and arranging.

The main ingredients of a good book on jazz history will be accurate definitions and explanations, a chronological order of the best players, and a choice discography. It is not likely that a single book can be used for all purposes. The most penetrating and thorough book is Gunther Schuller's *Early Jazz*.[2] Only in this book do we find extensive musical analyses of solos and arrangements, seen through the eyes, ears, and mind of an extremely knowledgeable performer-composer-author. His writing on Duke Ellington represents Schuller's finest effort and is indeed a masterpiece in jazz history. Schuller's compositions, especially in jazz, have reflected a potent Ellington influence as well, which presents a convincing argument for the virtues of researching the solos and compositions of a favored artist in order to assimilate his best qualities.

On an easier level of comprehension, yet especially accurate, is Charles Boeckman's *Cool, Hot, and Blue*.[3] Owing to Boeckman's conciseness and clarity in language, his judicious appraisals of players of *all* styles, and a prevailing attitude of openness and honesty, the book should outlast many of its competitors and is highly recommended.

Strangely enough, the best definitions of jazz and its position in thought and practice are contained in a book by a German, Joachim E. Berendt, entitled *The New Jazz Book* (translation by Dan Morgenstern).[4] The chapters called "The Dialectic of Modern Jazz" and "A Definition of Jazz" are especially fine. Morgenstern has also added an excellent discography at the end of the book.

I like Andre Hodier's *Jazz: Its Evolution and Essence*[5] for the categorical names and dates given to different eras in jazz and for its musical insight in certain areas, though I feel Boeckman's book is a better overall text. The most widely

---

[2] New York: Oxford, 1968.
[3] Washington, D.C.: Luce, 1968.
[4] New York: Hill and Wang, 1962.
[5] New York: Grove Press, 1956.

used jazz history book for class purposes has been Marshall Stearns' *The Story of Jazz*[6]—this is good, if dry.

None of these books are current enough to be used for researching the modern era, all having been written between 1956 and 1968. However, if the student who approached Clare Fischer for advice is any indicator, perhaps the modern period will be included in most "traditional" listening. Boeckman wisely closed his book with an open-minded discussion of rock music, followed by the conjecture that because of the nature of the styles and attitudes, jazz musicians might begin hopping the stylistic fence. He wrote this at a time when prejudice against the rock style was running very high, and before groups like *Chicago* and *Blood, Sweat and Tears* were well underway. At present it is difficult to name a group in jazz that hasn't been influenced by rock, or a rock group that hasn't been affected by jazz.

If anything is to be gained by gazing at old photos of earlier jazz players, and I suspect that there is, then the most fascinating collection of such photos would be Keepnews and Grauer's *A Pictorial History of Jazz*.[7] For the most complete collection of the big band era (1930s and 40s), I would recommend George Simon's *The Big Bands*.[8]

I'm very partial to black players because I feel that every significant change in the jazz style has been the product of an innovative genius who was most apt to be black, among other things. Yet most authors of books on jazz are white. They are too knowledgeable to leave out such luminaries as Armstrong, Ellington, Young, Parker, and Coltrane, but

---

[6] New York: Oxford, 1956.

[7] Orrin Keepnews and Bill Grauer, Jr., *A Pictorial History of Jazz* (New York: Crown, 1955).

[8] New York: Macmillan, 1971.

often an unconscious prejudice will cause them to dwell on Shorty Rogers, Dave Brubeck, Herbie Mann, or even Glenn Miller and Guy Lombardo. This is at the expense of describing black musicians who may not have been as great as an Ellington or a Parker, but were more gifted or representative of the jazz style than many white players. The real injustice is that the black music experience is sometimes consciously or unconsciously soft-pedaled. If I noticed it on my own, being white, then it must be (and is) even more apparent to blacks. For this reason, and to help bring the jazz history study into clearer focus, I would suggest that every student, black or white, read Leroi Jones' *Black Music*,[9] and his *Blues People: Negro Music in White America*,[10] or Alan Lomax's *Mister Jelly Roll.*[11]

As a companion to all the books, articles, records, and pictures used in the study of jazz history, Leonard Feather's *Encyclopedia of Jazz*[12] and *Encyclopedia of Jazz in the Sixties*[13] are extremely helpful as references, with their biographies, photographs, and valuable information. Feather's other books are well worth investigation, especially *The Book of Jazz*[14] and *Encyclopedia of Jazz on Record*, a fine historical collection which he edited for Decca.[15]

You may not immediately enjoy all you hear in studying jazz history. But remember, unfamiliar sounds and styles require some time before much absorption can take place. Also, don't view jazz as elementary or unenlightened just

[9] New York: Morrow, 1968.
[10] New York: Morrow, 1963.
[11] New York: Grosset and Dunlap, 1950.
[12] New York: Horizon, 1955.
[13] New York: Horizon, 1966.
[14] New York: Horizon, 1957.
[15] Los Angeles: Decca.

because it is not recent. I had the great pleasure of knowing and hearing Sidney Bechet in his later years, and though he was one of the earliest jazz musicians, he was also one of the greatest, even in his sixties. Much the same can be said of Duke Ellington, who never failed to express music, as a player and a composer, at the very highest level of beauty and craftsmanship. Their genius was as real in the 1920s as it was at the end of their long and productive lives.

2

UNDERSTANDING
JAZZ STYLES

The gap between hearing a recorded solo and understanding it fully or being able to play it is great. Even listening more, and to all the best players, can't by itself close that gap, though it helps. Yet it is extremely important to come to an in-depth understanding of what is heard. Imagine a student who has heard many recorded solos and who knows all the possible chord scales and progressions. Perhaps he can even play indefinitely without playing a "wrong" note, but he still has many choices to make in each phrase he decides to play, and chances are great that he isn't ready to make them. Some of the "right" notes are "righter" than others, and only observation and experience will eventually enable him to make better choices and fewer choices, too, since good improvisers usually acquire a sense for economy (deleting unnecessary pitches) as they mature. Miles Davis is today perhaps the most skillful in playing economically—stressing fewer, but well-chosen, notes and also making better use of rests, a very potent musical device.

In order to know exactly what a recorded jazz artist has played, the student will inevitably need to study transcriptions (written notation) of recorded solos. This becomes his means of observing what others have played, assuming he is using the same kinds of progressions and chord scales to become such an improviser.

Although there are sources for solos that have already been transcribed, more benefit is derived if the student transcribes them himself. Such activity will develop the ears, attune the senses to *all* details of the solo (because it is heard more closely and more often), create a deeper understanding of the correlation between sounds and their written notation, improve technique, and build confidence. Nonetheless, the study of pre-existing transcriptions is also valuable as a learning experience. It has some further advantages, in that published transcriptions may be more accurate. Moreover, they give the student more examples to work with. In any case, it is advisable for any serious student to use both methods—write his own transcriptions and study pre-existing ones.

David Baker is one of the major sources of jazz transcriptions. He has transcribed many solos in a variety of instruments and styles, and published them in *Downbeat* magazine in recent years. He has also included transcribed solos in his *Jazz Improvisation*[1] and *Developing Improvisational Facility.*[2] Some of his compositions, like "Coltrane: In Memoriam," even incorporate transcribed solos. Baker has now begun a series of books entitled Jazz Styles and Analysis for different instruments. At this writing the first of the series, for trombone, has already been released.[3]

[1] Chicago: Maher, 1969, pp. 109–20.
[2] Volume I (Libertyville, Ill.: Today's Music, 1968), pp. 76–80.
[3] *Jazz Styles and Analysis* (Chicago: Maher, 1973).

Additional sources of transcriptions include other or earlier *Downbeat* issues—for instance, Dan Haerle's piano solo series, published in that magazine in 1971-72. Zita Carno transcribed nearly everything that John Coltrane recorded. Some of his work was printed in *Jazz Review* magazine (now defunct) in the late 1950s and might be located in a large library. Gunther Schuller has transcribed many solos for magazines and books, and his commentaries on those solos represent the birth of such in-depth jazz analysis. (Schuller was already publishing analyses of this sort in 1958, for *Jazz Review.*) A few collections of transcribed solos have been published, without analyses, and these can be found in larger music stores. *Downbeat* has been including transcribed solos in its issues off and on since the 1930s.

Learning to transcribe music is extremely difficult at first. It takes practice, more for some than for others, but eventually almost anyone can learn, and the benefits are great. Aside from the intellectual understanding, even more important is that in learning to transcribe the solos of others we better our chances of transcribing *our own* musical ideas as they present themselves during the course of an improvisation.

SPECIFICS FOR STUDY

In learning to transcribe and study improvised solos, I offer the following suggestions:

Transcribing solos

1. Decide what players you wish to investigate.
2. To start with, look for shorter and/or simpler solos.

3. Whenever possible, look for tunes for which you know the progression.

4. Be sure of the key. The reproduction pitch of individual phonographs may often vary by a half-tone.

5. If the recording is in stereo, shut off one side from time to time if it causes the soloist to be more easily isolated and heard.

6. Consider transferring the recording to a tape, thereby saving wear on the record and making it easier to return to a particular passage in the solo.

7. Play the tape or record at half-speed (e.g., 7½ to 3¾ ips on a tape or 33 to 16 rpm on a turntable). This lowers the pitch by an octave and reduces the tempo, making transcribing easier.

8. Use your instrument for most of the transcribing, rather than a piano (unless, of course, that is your instrument). If you do this even before you transcribe it onto paper, it will be both learned and transcribed more easily and should eventually lead to your being able to transcribe your own musical thoughts *spontaneously,* as in performance.

9. When it is time to write it down, mark off the exact number of measures used in the solo (use double bars for section indicators, if you wish) and write the chord progression over the appropriate measures. Then write out a stemless, beamless version that merely places the note heads in the correct measure. Finally, work on the actual note durations and add stems and beams.

10. When the written version of the solo is complete, check its accuracy against the recording and make necessary corrections. It may be helpful to return the player to the original speed at times, if it has been slowed to facilitate transcribing.

11. Play the solo along with the recording many times, observing and imitating with exactness the tone quality, phrasing, articulation, time-feeling, etc. When any of these items can be represented in notation, add them to the transcription—pitch succession alone does not tell the whole story. Memorize the solo, if possible.

Studying transcribed solos
(pre-existing and original)

1. Place a numerical digit (1–13) over each pitch of the transcription that shows the relationship of each pitch to the root of the chord assigned to that measure or beat. This will tell more about the pitch choices for all chords that were selected or heard by the soloist.

2. Look for consecutive digits that recur in another part of the solo, perhaps as a re-used pattern or a cliché.

3. Examine the phrase construction, rhythms of the phrases, and common intervals used, and look for clever overlapping of phrases that join two chords, sections of the tune, or successive choruses.

4. Try to identify the source of the ideas. Are there any motif fragments from the opening or melody chorus of the tune? Are there quotes from other tunes, other players' solos, or other solos by the same artist? Are there recognizable patterns or interval sequences? As well as some of the foregoing, there will probably be some unsuccessful phrases, chord-running phrases, scalar phrases, and linear (nonmelodic) sections. Hopefully, there will be a few (though not as many as you might expect) phrases which are new, creative, and original. Take special note of such phrases. They may help you discover what seemed significant to the recorded player as he listened to the playback.

5. Pay careful attention to the manner in which the player interprets altered dominant sevenths (e.g., chords containing raised or lowered fifths and/or ninths, or additions of elevenths or thirteenths).

6. Learn to compare two solos in analysis. Much can be learned from such comparisons if the pairings are carefully chosen. It could be two solos by the same artist on the same tune, perhaps at different stages of his career. It might be two different soloists playing the same tune on separate recordings, or even on the same record. There are many other interesting combinations to try, each showing a slightly different result.

7. Notice especially those phrases that please you most (aurally) and try to learn some of the reasons *why* they are particularly pleasing. It may have simply to do with the manner of instrumental performance (fast, pretty, good phrasing or sound, clean, etc.) or it may sound well for cerebral reasons (clever handling of materials). It may appeal to you for purely esthetic reasons (beautiful, swinging, "down home," driving, etc.), but you will still know what pitch sequences, rhythms, and the like were a part of that esthetic creation.

8. Learn the terminology of musical analysis, with which we can verbalize, compare, and think about solos. It can lead to a greater understanding and appreciation of all solos, including your own.[4] Below is a partial glossary of such terminology.

augmentation – increase in note durations, usually by doubling those durations, causing the musical phrase to last longer without actually changing the tempo.

blue notes – the three notes commonly associated with the blues idiom, which are the lowered third, fifth, and seventh intervals above the keynote.

change-running – arpeggiation of each chord in a progression (*change* is a slang expression for chords).

comping – rhythms played by a chording instrument such as piano, guitar, or organ.

contours – the shapes of phrases as determined by their motion up and down in pitch and the durations of the pitches.

density – thickness of the music, primarily determined by the number of notes involved.

diminution – antonym of augmentation, achieved by shortening the durations of notes, usually by half, causing phrases to last a shorter length of time without changing tempo.

economy – the quality of using as few pitches as possible without sacrificing meaning.

embellishments – pitches added for decoration.

---

[4] David Baker's *Arranging and Composing* (Chicago: Maher, 1970) has an excellent chapter called "Techniques to Be Used in Developing a Melody." Information on terminology and techniques of melodic development are also contained in Baker's *Jazz Improvisation* (Chicago: Maher, 1969).

extension – (melodic) gradual lengthening of phrases by adding notes to the end of them. (Harmonic) the use of added chord tones, such as ninths, elevenths, and thirteenths.

fragmentation – development of a musical line by focusing on brief segments of a given melody, usually resulting in a fair number of repeats and permutations of the fragments.

intensity – a measurement of strength, relentlessness, and tension as brought about by a variety of musical practices, such as volume, accents, tempo, density, tone, articulation.

getting outside – slang expression for deliberately (usually) moving away from order, consonance, and simplicity.

jazz intonation – a deliberate distortion or reorganization of the tuning temperament of this hemisphere, in evidence especially on *blue notes*.

linear – a musical line in which the melody can seldom be divided into smaller phrases. Phrase endings are largely absent and the rhythmic values are relatively constant, such as long, unbroken chain of eighth-notes.

polychords – incidence of two or more chords simultaneously.

rhythmic (or **metric**) **shifts** – entrance of a repeated phrase on another beat of the measure rather than in the initial phrase.

simplification – removal of extraneous notes from a phrase, leaving only the essential or skeletal tones.

sustained tension – generally unrelieved dissonance.

truncation – shortening of a musical phrase by removing notes from the end of the phrase. The phrase is usually repeated a number of times; more notes are removed with each repeat.

THE IMPORTANCE OF THE EAR

Because so much of our success as improvisers depends upon a "musical ear," this section will discuss the development and function of this phenomenon. Although some of the theories will seem unscientific and farfetched to nonmusicians, the special musical "sense" that good musicians develop is vital to understanding, improvisation, and composition.

The ear can be cultivated

Many believe that people are either born with a "musical ear" or not; and if not, there is little that can be done about it. This is not true and can be disproven in a number of ways. Achievement levels in the dictation that we usually find in a music theory course will show that while the level of difficulty increases, the grade curve remains about the same. Jazz musicians are usually at the top of the curve, too, because they have learned to use their ears in a more complete way than other types of musicians. Repetitious disciplines can train just about anyone to develop a musical ear.

The memory retains everything that has ever been heard

It may take practice to learn to tap such a vast memory source, but it's all there. Most of us can hear music in our minds that is not, for the moment, being played or reproduced in an outside source. Whole selections can be heard in the mind this way, indeed, even whole LPs with their sequence of selections and keys can be "played" in the mind. Often, we are not consciously aware that we are capable of this kind of memory-tapping. Each of us has had moments when we were unable to recall someone's name, for example, and said to ourselves, "I'll think of it," or "It will come to me later." Sure enough, after a delay of anywhere from a few seconds to a few weeks, the elusive name drops into our consciousness, though we have not been thinking about it since the moment when we were first unable to recall it. At times such as these, the subconscious mind relays the information to the conscious mind. Had we made a negative suggestion to ourselves at the time of the memory lapse, like "I'll never think of it" or "Gone forever," we might have hindered the effort of the subconscious to look it up for us.

It is equally fascinating that *we are able to remember even the portions that are not understandable to us,* such as the types of chords that are being used, complicated solos, and massively orchestrated scores. We remember the sound, whether we understand it or not. Furthermore, we can learn to use our musical memory like a tape recorder, putting it in rewind or fast forward position.

The ear continues to function in sleep

Most people are aware that courses have been published on records that are meant to be played and absorbed in sleep, although little has been done with music in this manner. But we can even work on music in our dreams. Once, when I was slowly transcribing a choice piano solo by Clare Fischer, I had a dream in which I found myself sitting at a keyboard. I arrived at a place in the solo where I had not, in my waking life, been able to find the precise chord voicings he used. In the dream I continued right through the troublesome passage. I became excited about the discovery and awakened. I went to the piano to check what I had played in the dream and to my astonishment the passage was now correct.

A precise pitch can be memorized

I first became aware of this fact while studying music theory in a class that was conducted by Dr. Roy T. Will. Dr. Will was a very well-organized sort of person who required that each student purchase an A-440 tuning fork and carry it with him at all times, listening to it as often as possible. At various points in his lecture, he would turn quickly to the class and ask us to sing A-440. At first our collective guess wasn't very impressive, but in a short while nearly everyone could remember and sing the pitch on call.

Any pitch can be raised or lowered slightly without becoming another note altogether. This is why musicians will tune up before playing—not to find the approximate pitch but the *precise* pitch (intonation).

I have often seen musicians who, taking their instrument from the case and without hearing another instrument, instinctively adjusted a tuning slide or mouthpiece after a few trial notes, sensing that they were flat or sharp in relation to some universal, more stable pitch. I also remember one instance in which a watch repairman challenged me to determine, without referring to an instrument or tuning device, the pitch of a watch that operated on a tuning fork principle. I was confused by the pitch, because it seemed to be *between* two semitones, so I answered that it was a pitch between two particular notes. The answer was correct.

By association, the ear can memorize infinitesimal differences in tone quality between one note and another, each related to a corresponding pitch

Although quality-pitch correlation can be developed on

virtually all instruments (Chet Baker, for example, used it with trumpet), the saxophone is a good example. Written C♯ on the third space (treble clef) is played on a saxophone by raising all fingers, which causes air to escape through the tone holes long before the sound reaches the bell of the instrument. The resulting quality is thin and nasal, compared to other notes. Yet when the saxophonist moves from that C♯ to a note that is only a semitone higher (D), he replaces nearly all the fingers to cover the holes in order to create that pitch. The resultant quality is hard and full, and *very* different from the C♯. Even the nonsaxophonist notices the difference quickly. This means then that if I promise to play only one of those two pitches on a saxophone, *everyone* will know which is which, because of the *quality*. It follows that all notes, because they are fingered differently, have slightly varying qualities which, with careful observation, can be used to determine *all* pitches. On brass instruments, notes have differing qualities because the brass tubing is longer or shorter, depending upon which valves or slide positions are used. Stringed instruments have various material compositions (metal, gut, wound, etc.) that affect the quality, and open strings are recognizable. Once the ears are trained to hear the quality differences and associate those qualities with particular pitches and/or fingerings, the player can begin to understand *spontaneously* what pitches he is hearing, either on a record or in his own mind. At that stage of development, he can also begin pre-hearing improvisations (practicing) without the instrument in hand, even creating new phrases, but always sure of the fingering and pitch. If he hears a different instrument than the one he plays—one on which he has developed quality-pitch association—he needs only to imagine each pitch being reproduced on his own instrument, and the ear and memory will come up with the corresponding quality for the pitch, as well as the fingering.

The ear can hear quality-pitch association
on additional instruments

Learning quality-pitch association on one instrument does not mean that the student will not be able to develop the same ability on a related or unrelated instrument, or on an instrument of different pitch and/or range. Why do you suppose that, say, an E♭ alto saxophonist who tries to play B♭ tenor saxophone for the first time in improvisation often finds himself a fourth or a fifth interval away from what he thought he was about to play? Obviously, his pitch sense on alto was well ingrained, yet in a short while the problem abates, because he begins to hear tenor pitch. His alto pitch need not be disturbed in the slightest by taking on a new set of pitches to be related to quality. I have studied a number of instruments of different families and different pitches and I have yet to study one for very long before the quality-pitch association begins to work. I believe this is true for all players, whether they are conscious of it or not.

The ear's memorization of quality is so exact
that fingering can be determined
even when pitch is faulty

A friend of mine once brought a Duke Ellington record to my home to hear a Ben Webster solo I'd never heard. Since it was a tenor saxophone solo, I wasted no time applying the quality-pitch association to what I was hearing. At first I was somewhat flabbergasted at his technical fluency in the key I was hearing. But then I realized that the qualities produced by the various fingerings were *not* matching the correct pitch. Because the fingering does not change, I presumed the pitch to be incorrect. Sure enough, we discovered that the record was playing a semitone higher than it was recorded, changing the pitch but not the quality.

The ear can be trained to quickly recognize any musical device that is widely used and heard often

If I play a major triad or a major scale, for example, for a group of students, nearly everyone will recognize the device by ear without having to re-hear and study it for several minutes. It is an example of quick recognition. The same can apply to many other devices, as long as an effort is made. Such a list would include intervals, chords, scales, inversions of chords, progressions, key shifts, chord spacing or voicings, patterns, familiar motifs, chord function, note-of-chord function, melody-to-key relationships, diatonicism, and chromaticism. It is the mark of a fine and well-trained musician to be able to quickly identify and use all such devices. Perhaps it is this ability that distinguishes the best from the merely good jazz artist.

The ear can be trained to pre-hear phrases, counterpoint, and harmonies that have not yet been played or written

Composers will often use this ability to "audition" music in the mind before it is committed to paper. The effect is complete, and without needing to go to, say, a piano, he knows what the phrase will sound like. He can even project the sounds of the instrumentation used in his orchestration.

In this chapter we have been discussing, basically, the understanding of jazz style that is necessary to reproduce and create this kind of music. Learning to transcribe the music of recorded artists is vital in developing this understanding. So is developing a musical ear by constant training. Perhaps it would be safe to say that any really good musician—particularly jazz musician—is made, not born.

3

JAZZ KEYBOARD

The piano is perhaps the most familiar musical instrument of the Western world. The guitar must run a pretty close second by this time, but it is piano that the universities insist upon as a secondary instrument for all nonpianists. It is still a standard item of furniture in homes, night clubs, hotels, recording studios, schools, and meeting halls, to mention a few, and it is still the instrument used by most composers, arrangers, and songwriters for their creative endeavors.

Traditionally, the piano has been used to acquaint the uninitiated with music, to increase their finger coordination, to teach the reading of the Grand Staff (treble and bass clefs), and of course to entertain guests with the performance of dazzling little parlor pieces. In the study of jazz, the need for an understanding of the keyboard is much greater, owing to the many ways in which we need to *use* the piano. The word "use" as opposed to "play" is emphasized here for good reason. It is one thing to study piano with the expectation of becoming a pianist and quite another to study piano for purposes of *using* it to reach a greater understanding of music in general, or for fulfilling nonperformance or light-performance needs in music.

The piano keyboard can be used by the nonpianist much as one uses a typewriter or a computer. Instruments of this nature are used by many for the purpose of solving problems and preparing manuscripts. The piano can be used by the nonpianist in much the same manner. Many instruments are not capable of producing complete chords or even harmonic intervals sounded simultaneously, nor are the fingerboards, valves, and slide systems of nonkeyboard instruments designed to permit *visual* understandings of intervals, chords, scales, voicings, progressions, and the like. The keyboard of the piano, however, not only will sound many notes simultaneously, but has keys that are arranged symmetrically throughout each octave. Many musicians visualize the piano keyboard in their mind when computing chord and scale structures, even though they may be saxophone, trumpet, or trombone players.

In order to determine how the subject of jazz keyboard should be studied, we need to consider the ways in which we plan to use it. Some of these are for

1. The sounding of new chords, scales, and progressions being currently studied
2. Ear training, especially in harmony
3. Preparation of keyboard accompaniment tapes for study in improvisation
4. Surveying collections of tunes in which melody and chord symbols are given
5. Communicating harmonic principles to an individual student or to a class (in teaching)
6. Sounding various voicings and alternate chords for consideration in composing/arranging

7. Demonstrating aspects of style and voicings to students (and professionals) who cannot cope with the music you've laid before them

8. Filling in for an absent or tardy pianist in a band large enough to need only minimal piano support

9. Accompanying students and singers or self

10. An important secondary improvising instrument

Most of the foregoing will be readily understood by most readers, but I should like to comment further on items 1, 2, and 10. The first two concern primarily our need to absorb and remember the various harmonic devices with which we are constantly confronted in learning to improvise and arrange jazz music. In recent years I have increasingly stressed individual keyboard work in both theory classes and jazz piano classes (for nonpianists), primarily for increased understanding of harmonic principles. It works to that end very well, but the real benefit is that the students learn to *hear* the harmonic traits and progressions, and quickly. It is far more efficient as a method of teaching harmonic dictation than by having the instructor play the progressions in class a few times. It is more efficient than study tapes, because the student is encouraged to think, feel, and *produce* the sound. The slower student generally requires more time to produce the sounds. Therefore he gives himself longer to consider and hear each sound, which is precisely the extra help he needs to solve his problem. Within a very short time after the initiation of the keyboard classes, harmonic dictation scores soar and the progress is faster in theoretical understanding as well as dictation. I shouldn't be surprised if, in the near future, all theory classes and fundamental jazz courses will take place in keyboard rooms, so that each student will have his own "computer" in front of him for a quicker understanding of every harmonic principle discussed.

Using the piano as an important secondary improvising instrument, students often find that they can more easily grasp both harmony and melody simultaneously in complex tune progressions. Without the piano, it is difficult to relate the improvised melodies of a single-line instrument to an unfamiliar set of harmonies. For example, a tune like Wayne Shorter's "Nefertiti" (recorded by the Miles Davis Quintet) would be difficult, if not impossible, to interpret in improvisation from melody and progression alone. Many of the chords are difficult to classify within the existing system of chord symbology. Even the chord scales derived from the given harmonies would not complete the picture. This is because the voicings, even in the simpler passages, of Herbie Hancock's piano work on that track are complex; yet they are indigenous to the tune itself and must be considered, even by the single-line improviser. Perhaps after a few bouts with "Nefertiti" at the piano (probably more than a few in this case), the nonpianist may be ready to return to his primary instrument and try to improvise against the learned progression that he now carries in his head.

Many jazz artists who are not pianists use and/or play piano. Some have even made recordings with notable success—Dizzy Gillespie (trumpet), Charles Mingus (bass), and Fred Lipsius (alto saxophone), to mention a few. And it would be difficult to find an arranger who doesn't use the piano, even though not all arrangers are pianists, to be sure.

Chord symbology

Nearly all the written music used in jazz-pop styles consists of chord symbols and/or melody and chord symbols (commonly referred to as "lead sheet" or "melody and changes"). It is relatively uncommon to find the chords written into the staves as a group of chord notes, except where the music has required specific voicings, as in "Nefertiti" or in Herbie Hancock's "Maiden Voyage." Sheet music for popular songs generally have an arrangement of the chord written into the staves, but most professional pianists and arrangers avoid using the exact voicings and rhythms shown in the sheet music, viewing them as somewhat simplistic and designed to accommodate the pianist who cannot understand chord symbology. Consequently, the student should investigate the various kinds of chords and chord symbols that are commonly used in the tunes he wishes to use as musical vehicles for playing, writing, improvisation, etc. Virtually any book on improvisation or arranging will include more or less complete listings of chord symbols, and the better ones will also include some of the alternate symbols for the same chords. Knowing alternate symbols becomes very important, because chord symbology is far from being standardized. For example, a minor seventh chord may be symbolized in any of the following ways:

mi.7
min.7
m7
−7

Selection of formula voicings

Even with an understanding of chord symbology, additional problems arise with the interpretation of those symbols in terms of spacing or voicing the notes implied by the symbols. There is seldom any reason to play a chord in its simplest form, a root-position stacking of the chord in one octave, 1–3–5–7:

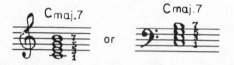

In nearly every instance, the notes of the chord will be spread over a range of anywhere from one and one-half octaves to three octaves. This is done by moving various chord tones into other octaves, creating pleasing vertical arrangements of the chord tones that are more effective than a simple 1–3–5–7 arrangement of those tones. This practice is commonly referred to as "voicing" a chord. A "formula" voicing would be a voicing arrived at almost automatically because the player has conditioned himself, through practice, to use the same voicing arrangement for many or all chords. This removes the need to consider, with each and every chord, exactly how it will be voiced, permitting him to move on to other problems. Obviously, one formula voicing (only) could quickly become almost as sterile as a 1–3–5–7 if there is no variety, so alternate formulas must be acquired in time. Also, it would be helpful if the formulas used early in the student's efforts were easy to find, reasonably simple, easy to finger and/or reach, economical in motion between one chord and another, and used voicings that would accommodate later adding of other, more interesting, chord tones and/or a melody. The following exercise illustrates the use of a formula voicing and can also be used, because of its consistent, parallel motion, as an exercise to help bring about the needed physical familiarization with the keyboard:

In playing something like this exercise, the student will not necessarily understand the chord structures he plays at first, even though he is successfully producing them through a system that is relatively easy to play. But in time, when the initial tasks become learned disciplines, the mind will be free to ponder *exactly* what is being played in terms of chord types, scale degrees, and even the voicings themselves. The student may not be aware at first where the various members of the chord can be found within a given chord and its voicing. But in a very short time, his *ears* will be able to distinguish such things and will aid him in finding the right notes for each of the chords shown in the exercise.

Playing the exercise in the key of C presents a minimal challenge, since only the white keys are used. The hands and fingers merely need to maintain their proper distances. Yet the exercise sets the student in motion, builds confidence, introduces him to chord types found on different scale degrees, and begins to expose his ears to particular arrangements of sound. After the exercise is learned in C, it should be learned in all other keys, eventually.

The student will be relieved to learn that the chord progressions to most songs use a surprisingly small number of chord types, and most of those are found on a very limited number of scale degrees within a given key. To be more precise, about 70 to 100 percent of the chords used in most tunes are II^{m7}, V^7, or I (M or m).[1] The tune may modulate to another key, but if the *new* keynote is thought of as I, the II^{m7}, V^7, and I of that new keynote will dominate.

Looking at the spectrum of chords shown in the exercise previously given (I–VII), the student can readily find II, V, and I and confirm that their respective structures (m^7, 7, and M^7) agree with what has been said about the commonly used forms of II^{m7}, V^7, and I^{M7}. It can also be stated here that those chords generally are found in the same *order* as given thus far—that is, II^{m7} is usually followed by V^7, and almost as often V^7 will be followed by I. If then, it can be anticipated that the progression II^{m7}–V^7–I^{M7} will occur often, it would be advantageous for the student to acquire a voicing formula for that sequence that would eliminate the unnecessary motion caused by playing all three chords as

---

[1] m = minor seventh chord. M = major seventh chord.

they appear in the 1–7–3–5 voicing of the first exercise. The excessive motion is even apparent to the eye in the following:

To avoid such skipping about the keyboard, a voicing formula such as the following example is suggested:

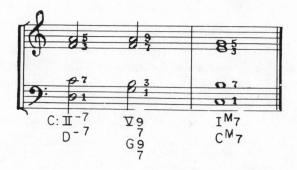

Not only is the above voicing formula for the II^m7–V^7–I^M7 sequence much easier to play, but it also creates a better voice-leading pattern (that is, the individual chord members of one chord move more gracefully into the chord members of the next chord). Also, by retaining one of the notes of the II^m7 (the fifth, A, is retained), the next chord, V^7, acquires a ninth, which adds color and interest to the sound of the V chord.

It was mentioned earlier that I follows V with somewhat less frequency than V follows II. This is because V often leads to a substitute for I, or returns to II, or moves to what would be II of another key or implied key. Therefore, the II–V progression should be practiced separately from the II–V–I, following some of the common II–V sequences as they appear in many tune progressions. The most common of these would be the II–V progression that progresses downward, as a II–V unit, by whole steps:

$$C : \text{II} - \text{V} \qquad B\flat : \text{II} - \text{V} \qquad A\flat : \text{II} - \text{V} \qquad G\flat : \text{II} - \text{V}$$
$$Dm7 - G7 \qquad Cm7 - F7 \qquad B\flat m7 - E\flat 7 \qquad A\flat m7 - D\flat 7 \qquad \text{etc.}$$

By following a key sequence C, B-flat, A-flat, G-flat, etc., the II–V *unit* progresses downward in whole steps. The individual *chord roots* actually move around the circle of key signatures (circle of fifths), [2] alternating between m^7 and 7 chords, but it will be found that it becomes unnecessary to ponder the V_7^9 chords after a while, because the two-chord formula (II leading to V) becomes a finger discipline that is somewhat automatic. In other words, it soon becomes as easy to play II–V as it is to play only the II, and little if any concentration is needed to find the V. Therefore the player arrives at the state where he is really only trying to find the placement of the II chord, letting the V chord take care of itself via the II–V unit voicing. The II–V unit moving

[2] The circle of fifths appears in the next section, Reading of chord progressions.

downward in half-steps is less common than this unit moving in whole steps, but it is prominent enough to warrant practicing of that pattern as well. Both patterns are illustrated below:

II–V Unit downward in whole steps

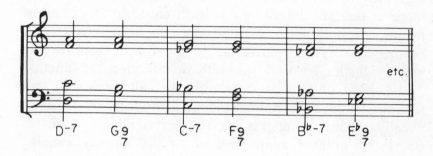

II–V Unit downward in half-steps

The II–V–<u>I</u> pattern also should be practiced downward in both whole steps and in half steps. Most students have little difficulty adding the I chord to the exercise after gaining control of the II–V progression.

Reading of chord progressions

As soon as the foregoing voicing formulas have been learned, it will be possible for the student to begin reading the chord symbols given for a vast number of tunes. Occasionally he may have to alter a chord tone as directed, such as lowering the fifth of a minor seventh chord, thereby forming the half-diminished seventh chord, or lowering or raising the ninth of the V7–9 chord to accommodate the occurrence of that particular form of the ninth in the melody. Such alterations generally do not affect the function of the chord, only its color. Nor are such alterations difficult for the student. A basic voicing formula, like 1–7–3–5, usually permutates quickly into the desired alteration. Sometimes the note is simply *added* to the already existing formula, as in the case of ninths, elevenths, and thirteenths. There is one problem encountered in reading progressions, however, that will require some extra attention on the part of the student. How does one know he is looking at a II–V or II–V–I unit when the symbols are given in *letters* instead of Roman numerals? Yet he must know the Roman numeral function if he is to know when he can economize on motion by utilizing a *unit* formula (like II–V or II–V–I) in his voicings. To help him with such determinations, he could:

1. Learn the circle of fifths, so that consecutive members of that circle can be recognized when they appear (as consecutive chord roots), since II–V and II–V–I patterns are based on the circle. For example, II–V–I in the key of C would be D–G–C, which are consecutive members of the circle of fifths.

2. Look for alternating chord types, like m7–7–m7–7–m7–etc., because this usually signifies a II–V pattern.

3. Look for chord types that might function as I (primarily major

Circle of fifths

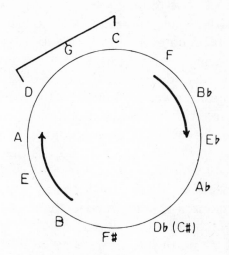

or minor triads and major seventh chords), hypothesize that the letter name is I, and look for supporting evidence of II's or V's in that area of the progression, both in terms of chord roots and the chord types present.

4. Practice II–V–I and II–V in all keys to become familiar with which *specific* lettered symbols are consistently grouped together.

Permutation and extension of formula voicings

As mentioned earlier, a basic voicing formula, like 1–7–3–5, can easily be altered or added to, retaining the basic part of the formula. Sometimes the chord progression asks for specific alterations or additions. At other times the keyboard player simply alters or adds notes to enrich the sound of the voicing, even if they are not specified in the chord symbols. He can do this as long as the changes made do not alter the function of the chords. The fifth (top of the 1–7–3–5 voicing) can be lowered or raised a half-step in 7 chords for color, or even raised a whole step so that it is no longer a fifth, but a sixth—or, more accurately, a thirteenth. Ninths can be added to the 7, m7, or M7 chords, and lowered and raised ninths can be added to the 7 chord. More than one alteration or addition can be made on the same chord. For example, a lowered fifth, a thirteenth, and a ninth (altered or unaltered) can appear together in a voicing like 1–♭7–3–♭5–13–9. Of course they should not be added if the note or notes collide with the melody.

To familiarize the hands with forming ninth chords, for example, the student might practice the following exercise (note that the retention of the top of the II^{m7}–9 chord causes a thirteenth to be produced in the V^7–9 chord):

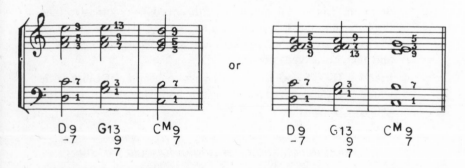

Another interesting way to capitalize on the learned II–V unit voicing is to use the same unit voicing formula for I–IV (both as M7 chords). Again, note that the retaining of the top note causes the IV chord to have a ninth. I–IV is not nearly as common as II–V or II–V–I, but it is nevertheless common enough to learn. Cal Tjader's "Liz-Ann," for example, contains five occurrences of I–IV (II–V–I–IV is the more complete progression that occurs), each in a different key, and the I–IV progression occurs frequently in the songs of Jimmy Webb.

Reading of melodies, accompanied by formula voicings

A good formula voicing should use as few notes as possible and still sound full or complete. One reason for this, given earlier, is to permit the adding of colorful tones, like ninths, elevenths, and thirteenths, without changing the basic structure of the formula voicing and without changing the function of the given chord. With only four fingers involved in the playing of, for example, the 1–7–3–5 voicing, other fingers can be used to add color tones. If the third and fifth of the chord were played by the thumb and forefinger of the right hand, then the second, third, and fourth fingers would be free to play other tones—or a melody. When the student has learned to play the chord progressions to a fair number of tunes by reading and interpreting chord symbols, the next logical step is to begin playing the melody as well, simply adding the melody notes to the learned voicing. At times it may be necessary to revise the voicing to accommodate a wide reach to a melody note or to delete a tone of the voicing because the melody has descended into the midst of the voicing. But it will also be found that the original voicing can be retained most of the time.

Expanded harmonic concepts

Although the reading of melodies and accompanying chord symbols for different tunes is certainly a worthwhile achievement, it still doesn't simulate very many of the keyboard sounds we hear in the playing of great jazz pianists like Herbie Hancock, Chick Corea, McCoy Tyner, or Keith Jarrett. In addition to their seemingly inaccessible virtuosity, their chording rhythms (comping) are more diverse and interesting than the effect gained by simply sustaining chords for their given durations. Their voicings sound more sophisticated and they utilize a wider variety of keyboard settings or background patterns. Listening and imitation will help the student to absorb some of the better comping rhythms, but the other two items will require that the student learn some new dimensions in his study of jazz keyboard. Not that we must compete with the masters, but we should at least increase our understanding and appreciation of some of the more accessible keyboard sounds used by such artists.

Most of the great pianists of the be-bop and post–be-bop eras of jazz, like Bud Powell, Thelonius Monk, Horace Silver, and Hampton Hawes, used voicings very similar to what has been suggested thus far in the exercises of this chapter. Their voicings, whether played with both hands or the left hand alone (as in accompanying right-hand improvisations) seldom failed to have the root of the chord at the bottom. Around 1955, however, Red Garland joined the Miles Davis Quintet and brought a new approach to keyboard voicing. He omitted the root from the bottom, if not altogether, placing instead a seventh or a third (usually) on the bottom, and played the voicings more in the middle and upper rather than the lower portion of the keyboard. Within a very short time, virtually all jazz pianists made a similar change, sometimes modifying Garland's exact voicings. It was plain to see that we were not going to be hearing many root-oriented voicings again, except perhaps in ballads or at important cadence points in faster selections. Rock music still emphasizes voicings with the root on the bottom, but the development of rock bass lines has sent that style searching for more inverted chords than have ever existed in the jazz idiom before Red Garland. And in the blues-oriented rock tunes, modern jazz piano voicings (with the third or seventh on the bottom) are heard frequently.

Given below is a sample of a very common voicing formula for playing rootless voicings (played by the left hand alone):

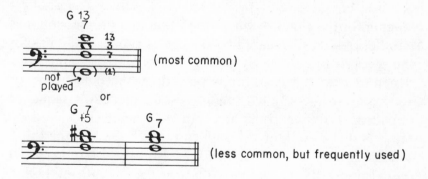

Note that as long as the seventh and third are retained, the top note can be used as a color tone, giving it the flexibility shown. The third and seventh can be reversed, as shown below, which causes the top note to be generally utilized as a ninth of some sort, rather than the thirteenth, augmented fifth, or fifth, as in the first voicings given.

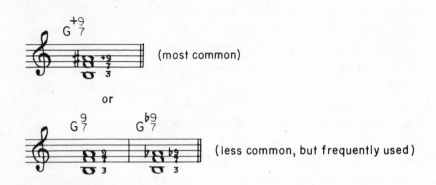

(most common)

or

(less common, but frequently used)

The 7 chord has been presented first in the discussion of rootless voicings because it is more representative in sound than are the rootless voicings for the m7 or M7 chord, which are less common and perhaps less effective. The rootless voicing for the 7 chord, when in motion in a progression, has another quality not shared by the use of rootless voicings for the m7 and M7 chord. It is two 7 chords at the same time, depending upon what note is played by the bass player or according to the implied tonality established by a sequence of chords. Looking at the first rootless voicing (F, B, and E), the F is the seventh of the implied root G, the B is the third, and the E is the thirteenth. But F is also the third of D-flat, B (enharmonically spelled as C-flat) is the seventh of D-flat, and the E is an augmented ninth to D-flat:
In other words, if the bassist plays a D-flat, or if the established tonality of the tune is D-flat, the first voicing (F,

B, and E) will be heard as a D-flat 7 chord rather than a G7 chord. Even if the color tone E is lowered to D♯ (enharmonically E-flat) or to D, the changed color tone will also fit the D-flat chord:

The interval between the third and seventh of any 7 chord is called, among other things, a *tritone* interval (because it measures three whole steps). This is a musical item given much attention throughout the history of music by all composers and theorists. Considering the two possible chord roots for the preceding voicings, G and D-flat, we note that they are also located a tritone apart. It is also true that a D-flat7 may be substituted for a G7 and vice versa. For example, the progression D^{m7}–G^7–C^{M7} (II^{m7}–V^7–IM7) could become D^{m7}–D-flat^7–CM7 (IIm7–♭II7–IM7), or the progression A-flat m7–D-flat 7–G-flat M7 (II^{m7}–V7–IM7) could become A-flat m7–G7–G-flat M7 (IIm7–♭II7–IM7). In other words, any 7 chords that are a tritone apart can be substituted for one another, a principle referred to by jazz musicians as *tritone substitution*. Often the jazz keyboard player (and the arranger, too) pull the preceding II^{m7} into the substitution principle just described, so that the progression D^{m7}–$G7$–$CM7$ becomes $A\flat^{m7}$–$D\flat^{7}$–C^{M7}.

Another aspect to this duality of roots that creates smoothness in voicing sequences is that a circle of fifths (in 7 chords) can be played *chromatically* downward. If we lower the first rootless voicing given (F, B, E) by one-half step, considering it, say, to be a G^{7}, we arrive at the pitches E, B-flat, and D♯ (or E-flat), which we *can* consider to be a G-flat7. But if the first chord was a G7, but also a D-flat7 at the same time, then the second chord can be G-flat7 *or* C7. Because C follows G in the circle of fifths, we can say that we have started around the circle of fifths by moving *down one-half step,* having the freedom to declare two different roots for any given 7 chord. In conclusion, if either of the rootless voicings given for the 7 chord is moved chromatically downward, there are *four* possible ways to define the progression, as given in the example below:

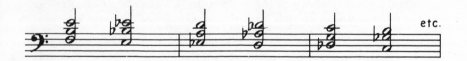

The above chromatic sequence may be combined with any of the following four bass lines:

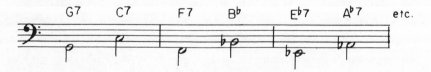

A good vehicle for working with rootless 7 chords is the blues, because they are often played with *only* 7 chords (on other scale degrees than just V), even on I, characteristic of the blues form. Another very strong characteristic of the blues is the frequently heard progression I7–IV[7]. These are two consecutive members of the circle of fifths and therefore playable *chromatically,* as shown before, except perhaps for the top tone, which may require a slightly different color. This is observable in the following left-hand exercise based on the blues progression, the E of the first chord moving down to a D in the second chord, rather than to E-flat— though the latter was still a possibility. A second version follows, illustrating the same progression in a different inversion, with the third on the bottom instead of the seventh (of the first chord). Both progressions are in G, although with only one mild change in the color tone of the second chord, both progressions can also be thought to be in *D-flat.* When the student begins to use the right hand for improvising a solo (and the blues would make a good vehicle for that, too), he should try improvising with the right hand in each of the two keys, using an almost identical left hand for each. It is good practice to create melodies that can solidify the feeling of a specific key, accompanied by something as ambiguous as the rootless, two-key left hand, because such improvisations lead to an understanding of how the various tones of chords and scales function within a given key.

One thing that has not been said about the desirability of using rootless voicings in general is that such a voicing does not inhibit the needed free motion of the bass line, which may at times use tritone substitutions whether or not they are also being used by the keyboard player. Voicings with the root on the bottom somewhat force the bass line to follow suit. This also creates intonation problems between the bassist's notes and the bottom of the root-oriented voicings of the keyboard, where there will exist many unisons that are unlikely to be perfectly in tune.

Shown below are two voicing formulae for the II^m7, V^7, and I chords, which again are *unit* voicings, like those used in the 1–7–3–5 voicings earlier in the chapter. Therefore they can be practiced in much the same fashion, as II–V or II–V–I units moving downward in whole steps and in half-steps, adding a right-hand improvisation to the exercise when the left-hand pattern has become learned. It would also be advisable to read all the same tunes that were used to practice reading progressions, using the 1–7–3–5, this time with rootless voicings instead of the root-oriented voicings. And it will be easier than before to add the written melody, because the left hand is now a self-sufficient unit, harmonically, freeing the right hand completely to play melodies or improvised melodies. Note in the given voicings below that either the third or seventh are once again on the bottom of the voicing, though we are now looking at m^7 and M^7 chords rather than 7 chords.

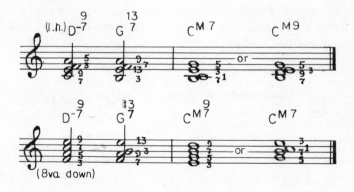

Miles Davis has furthered the career of many exceptional musicians by inviting them into his groups and into his awesome presence. But no less important is the fact that Miles has remained the focal point of the jazz idiom for over twenty-five years, spanning a time period that began with his close association with the legendary Charles Parker (Bird), probably the most influential player in jazz history, and up to and including his present rock-oriented group! During all that time, he didn't merely change *with* the times (with regard to style), but was largely—if not completely—*responsible* for most of the changes. One such innovation of the Miles Davis group of the mid-50s was the *modal* jazz style, introduced in the LP, "Kinda Blue." Several of the ancient modal scales were explored, but the one that really "stuck" was the Dorian mode. The structure of this mode may be examined by playing a C major scale from D to D (D–E–F–G–A–B–C–D). This is termed a Dorian mode on D, or simply D Dorian. The scale can of course be constructed on any pitch, using the signature of the key that is a whole step below the root of the Dorian scale.

In modally oriented progressions, the most obvious fact is that there are very few, if any, changes of harmony. Instead, a single chord scale might occupy at least eight to sixteen measures consecutively. Players who were accustomed to improvising by playing a few notes of each of the rapidly changing chords (called "change-running") suddenly found themselves hard-pressed to think of enough notes to play for those long durations in modal tunes. Their melodic concepts had to be changed and enriched. Likewise, the keyboard player could hardly sit there and play nothing but, say, a D^{m7} chord for sixteen measures or so, even with the use of all the alternate voicing formulas and permutations of those voicings. Besides, *each* time through the progression, during many solo choruses, those long durations remain to be worked with for perhaps 1,000 measures! If the next tune played is another modal tune, or if modal tunes are played every night in performance, it's easy to see that the keyboard player's concepts of voicing must also change at these times.

Perhaps the most famous of the selections found on the "Kinda Blue" LP was "So What." It introduced a voicing for the Dorian mode that is now often referred to as the "So What" voicing. Actually it is one voicing used in two different places in the mode, so that the keyboard player has two vertical chord sounds for each mode occurrence, with each using only available tones from one Dorian scale. Both vertical combinations use some other note than the root of the scale or chord on the bottom. It was found, in modal playing, that the long durations made it unnecessary to consistently reinforce the chord scale's root or even the tones of the m^7 chord by repeating them endlessly and redundantly. If those notes weren't played by the keyboard, then perhaps they appeared in the bass line or in the soloist's improvised line. If nothing else, those notes would still ring in the ear uninterruptedly from some previous measure. The "So What" voicing is given below, in the rhythmic pattern used on the record:

Even the above settings for the D Dorian were not enough, though. First side slipping occurred (independent chromatic shifting of the whole voicing up or down by half-step, against the constant, the *given* chord scale, reinforced by the other instruments). Then the "So What" voicing began to be played on each step of the key, even

those steps on which the intervals had to be slightly altered
to fit the key used by the mode:

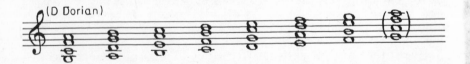

Because the perfect fourth interval plays prominently in
the structure of the "So What" voicing, and because the
voicing is difficult to play with the left hand alone, as in
accompaniment to a right-hand solo, the third interval at the
top of the voicing was often omitted. This led to quartal

harmony—harmony based on the perfect fourth interval. Then as a final step to freedom, pedal point was added. This is a musical device in which a functional tone, like a keynote or its dominant, is sustained in the lower register (often in octaves). At the same time, the right hand moves freely, though usually in parallel motion, to any note or chord from any key. Almost any combination sounds reasonably well, and the sustained pedal tone holds the actual key in focus. The chords often move chromatically down or up, sometimes in consecutive minor third intervals. The chords can be tertian (built with third intervals) or quartal. For an excellent example of both freely moving "So What" voicing and pedal point, listen to the end of McCoy Tyner's piano solo, just before John Coltrane begins his solo in "Pursuance," from the Coltrane LP "A Love Supreme." All the voicings and devices are used heavily by performers like Hancock, Corea, Tyner, and Jarrett.

There are several books that can be recommended for further expansion into the subject of jazz keyboard. A book that emphasizes "pop" harmony (generally rock), rather than jazz, is Mitch Farber's *Developing a Complete Harmonic Technique*.[3] John Mehegan's multi-volumed set, *Improvisation*,[4] is also extremely helpful—particularly Volume IV, which is devoted to prominent piano styles in jazz. My book, *Improvising Jazz*,[5] has a chapter devoted to functional harmony (Roman numeral translation of lettered symbols), an appendix on rootless voicings for piano, and 83 chord progressions for reading. *Jazz Improvisation* by David Baker[6]

[3] Ossining, N.Y.: Farber, 1970.
[4] New York: Watson-Guptil, 1959.
[5] Englewood Cliffs, N.J.: Prentice-Hall, 1964.
[6] Chicago: Maher, 1969.

is a highly recommended book on improvisation that has a chapter devoted to the keyboard. Another must for pianists is Dan Haerle's *Jazz/Rock Voicings for the Contemporary Keyboard Player.*[7]

Right-hand improvisations with left-hand accompaniment

Much has already been discussed and suggested concerning the activities of the right hand, particularly regarding rootless voicings. With the earlier pianists, like Bud Powell, the 1–7 portion of the 1–7–3–5 voicing was often used as a bare but sufficient left-hand accompaniment. Even the lowest two notes in the II–V unit voicing were frequently used. Horace Silver's nimble, lengthy fingers permit him to play 1–7–3 with the left hand alone, and with remarkable clarity. The rootless voicings and quartal structures make up the bulk of modern pianists' left-hand accompaniments to right-hand improvisations. The blues progressions are an excellent place to get started, graduating to harder progressions and modal tunes as the left hand becomes disciplined and the right hand loosens up for less inhibited performances. The following chapter, on improvisation, will provide suggestions for the development of the improvising right hand.

[7] Lebanon, Ind.: Studio P/R, 1974.

4

JAZZ
IMPROVISATION

Sometimes poetry, art, music composition, drama, and dance have been expressed spontaneously. There are improvising poets and actors. There is an Oriental style of painting that is improvised, with the brush never leaving the painting from the first stroke to the last. There are interpretive dancers who improvise, and of course most popular dancing styles are improvised by everyone. There have been some classical compositions that have incorporated improvisation into the music, especially in modern styles. We know that most of the traditional masters improvised often, at times for an audience, at other times to solve the mysteries of the next few measures of a piece that was being written. But the jazz idiom has stood virtually alone, for the better part of the twentieth century, in the utilization of improvisatory practices as its *focal point.* "Watching someone improvise in jazz," my wife put it once, "is like watching someone think on his feet." [1] And it is also like watching someone *feel* on his

[1] A play on words often used to describe the improvising wit of a lawyer or debater in action.

feet. He may have prepared for the present moment for many years. Indeed, the trained listener can spot an artist's clichés (something *all* artists have, not just improvising jazz musicians), but the essence of his solo is not predetermined. His thoughts and feelings of the moment greatly determine whether the solo is pretty or ugly, structured or free, intense or serene, etc. Its musicality is somewhat assured by experience and study, but pitch choices, motive fragments, and the general content and mood reflect the present moment and no other. Thanks to Edison, we can capture and catalogue such performances as they occur.

If we think of the jazz style as having begun roughly around the turn of the century, then it is surprising that the first significant books to teach jazz improvisation did not appear for about sixty years. My generation, and those before it, learned by trial and error and by asking questions of performers. Sometimes the answers had to be gained solely by listening and watching—and remembering. Few jazz players were formally trained in music theory and many were proud to say that they played "by ear," because they were somewhat suspicious that theoretical training might stifle the excitement and mystery. Even today, there are prominent musicians and educators who don't believe that improvisation can be taught. It may be that any performer or writer who is verbally articulate and who has the ability to organize methods for development is morally obligated to give information—information which, through experience, has been tried and proved effective. Those of us who became the first teachers have continued to write and have been joined by many others. One of the most prolific of these is performer/writer/teacher/composer David Baker. His outpourings in jazz-related materials are broad in scope and are excellent.

Learning improvisation is much like studying theory and composition. They have nearly identical ingredients with respect to available chord structures, scales, and the like. Even form is studied in much the same manner, as is counterpoint, but all under the heading of improvisation. The most significant differences between studying improvisation and studying theory and composition are that the information is taken up at a greatly increased rate (because much of it is needed immediately) and it is all applied to an instrument. For most music, the composer writes the piece and then the performer plays it when he is ready. The improviser, however, creates and performs simultaneously—*now*. In order to do so to any degree of success, the improviser must learn to transcribe what he hears, translating heard pitches into notes and/or fingerings. Chapter 2 discusses at some length the means by which we learn to hear more finitely, such as pitch-quality correlation. Time and experience play a very important role in the development of the ear, too, in meeting the needs of the improviser. Chiefly though, it is a slow building of associations between given harmonies and particular note sequences or patterns that must be continued until the improviser becomes a near-perfect transcriber of his own musical thoughts, at least, if not those of others.

PRESTUDY CONSIDERATIONS

Improvisation is a very challenging craft, mentally and physically, but especially mentally. The mind must be able to concentrate on many factors simultaneously, such as chord-scale structures, motif development, form, intensity level, absorption and use of musical ideas heard in the accompaniment, rhythmic levels and feelings, and so on. Because of this, the mind has little time to focus on aspects of instrumental playing, like embouchure, fingerings, technique, sound, intonation, breathing, and the like. Instrumental disciplines should be relatively ingrained through daily practice so that the mind needn't be constantly distracted by instrumental problems in subsequent improvisation sessions, but will be free to ponder the *content* of the solo. With the physical ease afforded by practice comes a more open channel for inventive or creative flow. More and more is then available to the innovator.

Although it is difficult to draw a line between instrumental preparedness and the lack of it, there are a couple of ways to determine whether or not an instrumentalist is ready to begin the study of improvisation. Because most improvisation takes place at the eighth-note level, and because the tunes and recorded accompaniment are at a medium tempo, at least, it could be said that a player probably shouldn't tackle improvisation until he has enough technique to play a rather continuous string of eighth notes at a minimal medium tempo. Another indicator is the ability to play a written-out solo of a recorded improviser. Age is not a significant factor, but instrumental ability is.

SPECIFICS FOR STUDY

In studying jazz improvisation, the student should involve himself in these activities (arranged in logical sequence):

1. Chord-scale symbology and nomenclature
2. Chord scales applied to instrument
3. Chord-scale patterning
4. Application of melodic (or scalar, digital) patterns to progressions
5. Playing experience with accompaniment (recorded or live)
6. Jazz keyboard (for nonpianists) (Chapter 3)
7. Solo transcriptions (Chapter 2) and listening (Chapter 1)
8. Melodic development and interval studies
9. Extended chord-scale study
10. Study of free form and extramusical devices

Chord-scale symbology and nomenclature

The identity of most tunes used for improvisation is the chord progression, which is generally rendered in symbols or called by name. This must be learned as early as possible so a person can function as an improviser. It requires an understanding of the symbols and the names for chords and scales. Although it is true that there are a number of alternate symbols for the same chords being used by different musicians, the alternates are not so numerous that they cannot be quickly learned. Nearly all books on improvisation include an early section that is devoted to symbols and nomenclature, and the better books also list at least some of the alternate symbols. For this purpose, I would suggest to the student either *Improvising Jazz*[2] or *Jazz Improvisation.*[3]

---

[2] Jerry Coker, published Englewood Cliffs, N.J.: Prentice-Hall, 1964.
[3] David Baker, published Chicago: Maher, 1969.

Chord scales applied to instrument

Although an understanding of chord scales is necessary, its helpfulness is limited until the information is channeled through the instrument, because a physical conditioning and a sharpening of reflexes is also necessary. At this point the student should make it a point to learn at least the major scale in all keys, if not the minor and modal scales as well, and perhaps even some basic chord-running (arpeggios) on major and minor triads and seventh chords. A tune can be in almost any of the twelve keys, despite the relative commonness of, say, C, F, or B-flat. Rock groups often prefer "open-string" (guitar) keys like E, A, D, and G. More traditional bands, like those of Basie and Ellington, favor flat keys through D-flat (five flats), and singers select keys according to range and desired brilliance, which could be almost anywhere. Even if a tune is played in a simple key, there are likely to be chords within the progression that derive from some very remote key, so there is no escaping the fact that knowledge of *all* keys is needed.

Chord-scale patterning

Playing up and down chords and scales is not a very imaginative form of improvisation. We need to search for *economical* ways to realize the chord symbols—that is, to imply chords and scales without necessarily playing *all* the tones inherent in the symbol. This may involve playing all the tones, but in a less predictable order and/or direction. Such devices often become what we refer to as *patterns.* Pattern playing is extremely important to the development of the improviser for a variety of reasons. Patterns introduce the player to nearly every new theoretical device, from the beginning of his study to the most advanced state. Patterns are used by every major player. The practice of patterns trains the ear to hear and understand *groups* of notes and groups of chords in a progression. It goes without saying that pattern playing also increases finger technique. Eventually, pattern playing begins to occupy the space (in a solo) between more important musical events, for the advanced player. However, patterns can still be very exciting at times, and their value to the beginning improviser cannot be overestimated. At first the student might simply play, for example, scales in thirds (e.g., C–E–D–F–E–G–F–A–G–B–A–C–B–D–C) or in broken scales (1–2–3–2–3–4–3–4–5–4–5–6, etc.). Patterns can be extended to cover the full range of the instrument. Sequences of chords and scales could be practiced that conform to common chord-root motions, like around the circle of fifths, chromatic motion, or up and down in whole steps or minor thirds. Digital fragments of chord scales, like 1–2–3–1, 1–2–3–5 (a pattern that John Coltrane used approximately thirty-five times in his solo in "Giant Steps") or 1–3–5–3 can be treated in the same manner with respect to common chord-root progressions.

There are several satisfactory books of patterns, the most extensive being *Patterns for Jazz*,[4] which contains 326 patterns in an order that goes from simple to complex and covers virtually every type of chord, scale, or harmonic device. Baker has authored several fine pattern books in a series called Developing Improvisational Technique,[5] with

[4] Jerry Coker, James Casale, Gary Campbell, Jerry Greene, published Lebanon, Ind., 1970.

[5] Chicago: Today's Music, 1968 (book is separately published from Russell's *Lyd. Chrom. Con.*, but subtitled "Based on the Lydian Chromatic Concept).")

separate volumes devoted to the II–V[7] progression, turn-backs, cycles, and a supplement to George Russell's *Lydian Chromatic Concept*.[6] Jamey Aebersold has produced several excellent accompaniment records, each containing a booklet on improvisation that includes patterns. *Patterns for Saxo-phone*[7] is a fine collection of patterns; however, there are no symbols or explanations to tell you what you are practicing or where you can use it, so it can only be recommended for more advanced students who are aware of such things.

It is important for the student to realize that the practice and use of patterns is merely to discipline him to become familiar with the possibilities and best choices of notes to be played against various chords. The patterns should build, enlighten, and extend the improviser's efforts, not restrict them. Pattern practice should probably be continued throughout the improviser's playing career. He should continually add new patterns, especially for the purpose of understanding and putting into practice the various new theoretical principles encountered (such as practicing dimin-ished scale patterns to learn the diminished scale itself).

Application of patterns to progressions

At this point the student should begin collecting the chord progressions for a variety of tunes, to be used as vehicles for pattern application. It is not too difficult to locate sources. Most musicians, especially leaders and arrangers, are likely to have "fake" books (legal and illegal), sheet music, and hand-copied progressions from which you can make copies or gain information about ordering your own.

[6] New York: Concept, 1959.
[7] Oliver Nelson, published New York: Noslen, 1966.

Surprisingly enough, it is easier to begin with fast-moving chord progressions—not in the sense of tempo, but using chords of short duration, say two beats for each chord, as in "Giant Steps" or "Countdown" by John Coltrane (at a much slower tempo, of course). One might think that it would be easier to use longer durations at first, to give the player more time—but time to do what? To discover just how difficult it is to find melodies and pleasing intervals while playing—all this without losing the place or mistranscribing the next phrase you're trying to hear? Or to make you aware of how much you're missing by not having five to ten years of experience and not knowing all the great solos that have been played? In other words, an improviser just getting underway is not likely to be ready for a lyrical-melodic concept of playing. He is more of an observer than a creator for the moment, and needs to be let off the creative hook while he does his musical pushups and rids himself of his self-consciousness, preparing for a better day. At this stage he may not need accompaniment yet, though it is always helpful to hear the chord played by a keyboard as he works with even simple patterns. Another reason it is easier to begin with progressions having chords of short duration is that the player is forced (for now, anyway) to use short and easily remembered patterns, such as a 1–2–3–5 pattern played in four eighth notes to encompass the duration of a chord lasting only two beats. The pattern would have to be played twice to accommodate a chord lasting four beats. Or an eight-note pattern could be devised (e.g., 1–2–3–4–5–3–2–1), but that would involve the memorization of a longer pattern. Some difficulty may be encountered in the attempt to transpose the pattern to each new chord root and chord type in a steady tempo, but that will soon pass.

After it becomes relatively easy to use, say, a 1–2–3–5 pattern to the progression of "Giant Steps," it is important to begin mixing patterns, alternating between several short patterns on successive chords. On chords of longer duration —say four to eight beats—a longer pattern, or an entire scale, or a brief melodic quote from another song might be inserted, just to familiarize the player with the molding of melodies and lines and to make his mind more agile. During chords of longer duration, the player can eventually try something extemporaneous, leaning on preconceived patterns during the other, faster-moving sections of the tune.

Finally, other patterns, especially longer ones and semimelodic patterns, should be explored, perhaps in progressions having slightly longer chord durations. Jerome Kern's "All the Things You Are," John Coltrane's "Moment's Notice," and Charles Lloyd's "Forest Flower" are good examples of tunes which contain mostly chords of four-beat durations. Two-measure and four-measure patterns can be used, also, provided that the chord durations are right, or that the player learns to adjust to a chord change that falls in the middle of a pattern.

Playing experience with accompaniment

Experience is very important to the student of improvisation and cannot be overemphasized. Every chorus played, even an unsuccessful one, is another source of growth. A great deal of time is needed—for making mistakes, for learning to hear, for solving problems, for developing strength, and for becoming consistent. Playing without accompaniment won't be enough at this stage, either, because an accompaniment makes the player more aware of his needed disciplines and eventually becomes an important source of his creative inspiration, when he can give it his attention. Playing experience with live accompaniment, especially early in study, is unfortunately very hard to get. One answer to this problem lies in Jamey Aebersold's previously mentioned accompaniment records. Volume I is called *A New Approach to Jazz Improvisation*, Volume II is titled *Nothin' but Blues.* Volumes III and IV have now been released. III is *II–V^7–5 Progression*, and IV is *Movin' On.* Still more are on the way. Aebersold's volumes have outclassed all similar such efforts of the past. The level is accessible to the average student, the booklet is concisely and well-written, and the "selections" (some are actually practice progressions) are appropriate and discerning. Moreover, the recorded players are superb individual musicians, and the sensitivity and inspirational quality of the rhythm section's accompaniment is excellent. The recording itself is well-produced, with thoughtful tracking that makes it possible to eliminate piano or bass, if the student plays either. There should be a prize for this sort of contribution to the field.

Needless to say, the Aebersold volumes are highly recommended to all students of improvisation, from beginners to advanced players. (Volume IV, incidentally, is extremely challenging to even the most advanced players.) Of course there is the need to play with a live rhythm section that can respond to what you play in a way that the recording cannot. But the unusually good quality of the Aebersold volumes is quite a lure, if you've only a poor rhythm section (live) to play with, or none at all.

This stage of learning is long and important to the student. It represents the springboard to more creative playing, and it will continue until the student has "put his bag together" and then some.

Jazz keyboard (for nonpianists)

If the reader has not worked with the materials in Chapter 3, perhaps this is a good time to do so. Such study is of great help in learning to understand and hear various chord structures and progressions. It is not as easy to accomplish this by practicing arpeggio chords and progressions on an instrument that only produces a single tone at a time.

Solo transcriptions and listening

The point to be made here is that by the time the student is ready for transcription, he is having to think less about technical aspects of improvisation (chords, scales, etc.) and is beginning to look about for some especially good players to listen to. He is now more ready to hear, understand, appreciate, and absorb some of the finer qualities of a good player. Furthermore, transcribing solos effects a great improvement in the ear, which is essential to transcribing musical *thoughts* as well.

For the same reasons, this is also a logical time to step up general listening (not necessarily with transcribing). Investigate discographies such as those found in *Patterns for Jazz*, *Jazz Improvisation*, Aebersold's record-accompanying booklet, or a reliable book on jazz history. Find out what others are listening to, especially if they are successful players. We are *all* a product of what we hear, after all. Finally, look over Chapter 1 for more suggestions.

Melodic development and interval studies

The study of melodic development solves problems and lends cohesion to a player's solo style. It also sensitizes the eyes and ears to the presence of melodic fragments (in an improvisation *or* in the given tune) that are especially appropriate to develop. The improviser needs practice to develop and transpose such fragments. And because melodies are made of intervals, sometimes having their very identity in certain of those intervals, it is also helpful to begin practicing patterns that are based on particular intervals. The interval of a fourth is a very popular interval at this time, for example, both in melodies and in improvisations.

Studies in melodic development may be found in *Improvising Jazz* and in *Jazz Improvisation*, already cited. Baker's *Arranging and Composing*[8] is also an excellent source.

Patterns for Jazz contains a lengthy segment of interval-based patterns. Such patterns are not difficult to invent and are interesting to study, in terms of discoveries of musical symmetries.

Extended chord-scale study

Any set of materials or patterns can become restrictive or dull after a period of time. The player should constantly search for new ways to handle his materials, with respect to patterns, new scales, new chords, etc. If he tires of, say, playing major seventh chords and major scales, he might try raising the fifth of some of the chords, creating a fresher

[8] Chicago: Maher, 1970.

chord structure (which still functions in the needed way). This new structure is an augmented major seventh chord (1–3–♯5–7), which uses an augmented scale, an interesting and new scale with which to work. There are always substitute chords and scales to explore.

Perhaps the most interesting and divergent book relating to chord scales and the like is George Russell's *Lydian Chromatic Concept*. Russell's unique system classifies, by relative consonance and dissonance, various scales (some original, some borrowed from tradition) in such a way that the user is able to control the consonance-dissonance factor in the content of his solos and at the same time inject freshness to the sound of the scales. As a tangential study, especially, this book is the most original approach to improvisational materials that has been published. As stated earlier in this chapter, David Baker has written a pattern book supplement to Russell's *Lydian Chromatic Concept*.

Baker's *Jazz Improvisation* is a thoroughgoing reference on chord-scale possibilities and both of my books (*Patterns for Jazz* and *Improvising Jazz*) also contain information on the subject. Baker's book and my *Patterns* book contain discussion and/or study of some of the Russell scales, in particular one that Russell has called the Lydian augmented scale.

Study of free form and extramusical devices

I am a firm believer that free-form music should not be played by less knowledgeable and less experienced players, at least not for very long. Two notable related quotes come to mind in this regard. Lee Konitz (jazz saxophonist) said "You've got to learn to play far-in before attempting to play far-out," and composer Bernhard Heiden said of a long, dull, free solo, "One *has* to play very well indeed to play for such a long time." Free-form music should for the most part be played by the very best players, whose long experience and study better qualify them to weigh and judge the inclusion of this phrase or that. Only these players have had the time to develop the presence of mind to listen to others in the group and join them in creating a unified concept of free-form music.

The term *free form* is, in most cases, a misnomer. Too much collective effort is involved to call it free. In most cases, free form means a performance without a prescribed chord progression. But in the best of so-called free-form recordings, we find elements like steady tempo (or tempi), often a regular, consistent meter, and just as often a sort of tonic tone in the bass line and/or in the solo. There are likely to be, as well, some developing of motifs contained in the melody to the tune or original motifs, and perhaps a couple of written finite ensemble choruses. There is a sense of accompaniment-solo functions and collectively played dynamic changes, to say nothing of all the disciplines and limitations each player brings into the performance. Freer it is; free it is not, and that's the only sensible way to approach the subject. Without the hidden unities just mentioned, the music would have little value or appeal to anyone, even the players. As a matter of fact, it is *precisely* the judicious handling of such factors collectively that makes for a successful effort in free-form playing.

No one can really tell you *what* to play in a free style, though there are hints contained in the previous paragraph, but obviously the more you know and have heard, the better the result. Not knowing for sure what you will be moved to play next, you must be ready to play *anything,* if you can.

You may even be moved to use an extramusical device—that is, a sound that is not normally associated with the instrument, though it is played by the instrument. Sometimes it uses a vocal sound, a fingering device, altissimo playing, and so forth. Extramusical devices can, of course, be invented by the individual player but there is a good segment on such sounds for all instruments in Baker's *Jazz Improvisation.* Any such device may have to be practiced as much as scales and patterns, to gain control of it. As always, listening to good examples on record is essential to developing a feeling for freer playing. Remember that the reason for the name *extramusical devices* is that, though they are not quite under the heading of musical sounds, they should be *used* in a musical way. Otherwise the name might be *nonmusical* or *unmusical devices.*

TROUBLE-SHOOTING IN IMPROVISATION

Some years ago, before I began teaching at a university, I was forced, for economic reasons, to accept a position as a dictaphone repair trainee, with no prior experience in electronics. The fundamental experience I gained in that position was learning to trouble-shoot problems by logic. You couldn't simply say the machine didn't work—you had to find out why and apply a solution to the problem. In teaching improvisation, I find that the same principle holds true in regard to members of the class who are faltering in places. I can't simply shake my head in negation to what they've played. I have to know why, if I am to relieve their suffering. On the dedication page of Jeffrey Furst's *Story of Jesus* (based on the Edgar Cayce readings), he wrote, "For the Master, who has never given up on any one of us." I'd like to think that I aspire to that attitude with respect to my improvisation students.

The following chart for trouble-shooting in improvisation should prove useful, because the problems listed are the most common ones I've come to know in teaching improvisation over the years. It was almost a relief to me to learn that we all share most of the same problems in our development.

PROBLEM	SOLUTION
Inability to find right notes fast enough, even with a reference sheet at hand.	Study instrument more, because fingerings and/or positions may not be sufficiently ingrained. Also, work on sight reading so that reference sheet may be perceived more quickly.
Difficulty in execution, inability to keep up with accompaniment or relate to pulse.	Study instrument more, perhaps with a metronome. Practice reference materials more (on instrument) so that they flow, and be sure that they are worked up to at least the tempo of the expected accompaniment. Practice (with metronome) playing chord scales at each rhythmic level (in half-notes, in quarters, eighths, etc.), leaving metronome at one tempo only. Then focus on eighth notes for a while in your development.
Losing place in reading progressions, especially if chord durations are to be of varying lengths from, say, two beats to two measures.	Listen to a recording of the material repeatedly, with the reference sheet at hand, clapping, nodding, or tapping each time the chords change, studying the harmonic rhythm. Also, practice improvising at one rhythmic level, with accompaniment, using fewer rests for a while so that you may quickly compute how many notes are needed to consume any given chord duration. Use digital patterns of the same durations, if necessary. Finally, pay closer attention to the difference in sound of each of the chords and their placement in the progression, using the recognizable ones as sign-posts.

PROBLEM	SOLUTION
Though isolated chords are relatively easy to handle, difficulty is felt when moving from chord to chord.	There are relatively few kinds of chord motion, so practice the more common of these (cycle, chromatic, stepwise, in minor thirds, etc.), using patterns as a vehicle. Also increase technique on instrument (perhaps through increasing tempo of patterns practiced) so that the execution is assured. Learn to look ahead at next chord, find graceful chord connections (which increases awareness of the chord change) and consider treating some of the more significant chords more extensively than others.
Inability to hear progression when reference sheet is not at hand.	Repeat above solution. Work on materials of Chapter 3 (Jazz Keyboard) at a piano or organ. Study and memorize a number of progressions until you are able to see their similarities, which greatly outnumber their dissimilarities.
Unable to use melodies and other elements of style that were learned by ear prior to formal study.	*All* melodic fragments, patterns, etc., must be understood in terms of their implied harmonic setting (and some have more than one that is possible). Otherwise it cannot be known when to use it. The ear and the mind must be used collectively, because one is lost without the other. Find the harmonies for ideas learned by ear, past and present. Theoretical understanding will clarify and extend, not inhibit, creativity.
Even with understanding of reference materials, selection of notes and phrases is still too ambiguous to allow playing with any degree of confidence.	Transcribe a recorded solo to a known progression. Analyze by placing a digit above each pitch that shows the relationship of each pitch to its accompanying chord. Then review the analysis, noting the approximate frequency of the digits (how many roots, fifths, ninths, etc.?). Go over it again and look for digital sequences that are used more than once (e.g., 1–2–3–5). In observing the choices of more experienced players, the confidence factor should improve. Also, if the reference materials include only chords and/or scales, extend these materials into patterns and practice them until subsequent improvisations begin to include at least allusions to the patterns practiced. Patterns will, among other things, ingrain variously shaped mini-phrases that will lead to other, more creative phrases.

PROBLEM	SOLUTION
Style is indistinct and/or naive and execution lacks conviction.	Transcribe a number of solos by admired performers (ask, if too few of the more significant players are known) and play them frequently, especially with the recording, but also without. Take careful notice of the sound, phrasing, articulation, time-feeling, and, in general, the delivery of the recorded soloist, and imitate in greatest detail. Using a variety of good soloists will insure that your style is not completely dominated by one player, though many great players have remained under the spell of a single player for long periods of time. Oddly enough, no two players ever sound *exactly* alike, despite any effort to do so.
Bored with hum-drum phrases and limited note choices on reference sheet.	The chromatic scale (and more) can be used by the player who understands it sufficiently. But long before that, there are new patterns, substitute chords and scales, newer varieties in chord and scale structures (some from foreign cultures), rhythmic-metric-accenting devices, motive development, new and provocative progressions to explore, more players to hear, etc. When boredom threatens, turn it back with something new in the way of a discipline or an understanding.
Solo content lacks cohesion, seems aimless, and feels the same from tune to tune.	No two tunes are exactly alike. Each has its own combination of motifs, chords, tempi, measure structure, mood, etc. The improvising player should study and consider those elements, *especially* the distinctive ones, and use them as raw material for the solo, which should be a development of the tune and all that implied by it. Use the motifs, intervals, rhythms, etc. in free and fragmented developments during the solo, giving it both a direction and a distinctive quality. Be clever in your handling of these elements.

5

JAZZ ARRANGING[1]

In general, music should be written chiefly by the most gifted and thoroughly trained of our musicians. There are, of course, exceptions to the rule, but generally speaking, the musical demands for becoming a successful arranger are great. The arranger needs to have heard and remembered an enormous amount of music of many styles, past and present. He needs to have absorbed all the theoretical materials studied by the improviser (chords, scales, intervals, patterns, melodic development, ear training, etc.) and more (notation, scores, form, instrumental ranges, transposition, keyboard, voicings, orchestration, counterpoint, etc.). Contrary to popular belief, he should be a well-trained performer and improviser, perhaps playing several instruments, because such training can increase his understanding of performers and improvisers. The arranger also needs to possess one of the best sets of musical tastebuds, for his value judgments will affect many others. It also helps if the arranger is

[1] A distinction between *arranging* and *composing* is unnecessary, since it is inconceivable that arrangers cannot compose or that composers cannot arrange.

experienced in conducting rehearsals. Finally, dedication and good concentration are needed to carry him through the long and lonely hours he'll spend pushing a pencil.

PREPARATORY ACTIVITIES

The study of arranging requires patience. The first arrangement may not be possible until the necessary preparatory hours have been spent memorizing the multiplication tables of music, reading, listening, and observing. Many things need to be absorbed before the score can be attempted. Among them are the following six categories:

Listening

Learn to listen with your full attention, expecting to learn something new with each listening. Practice reading song collections with chord symbols at the piano, learning and memorizing some of the tunes. Learn what makes an attractive tune or chord progression—these are the raw materials of arrangers. Listen to different versions of some of the best tunes. Then begin taking notice of the details of arrangements, transcribing devices you'd like to remember, use, or paraphrase. Note that there seem to be different ways to approach the arrangement, not so much with respect to style, but with regard to overall structuring of arrangements. Regardless of their style, arrangers are likely to organize their work in a way that is appropriate to each particular tune progression used, and there is much variety. Three of the most common types of arrangements are:

1. A loosely written arrangement, utilizing small-group idioms (regardless of size of instrumentation), use of indefinitely

repeated motives and vamping figures, and leaning on improvisation, spontaneity, and editing.

2. The traditional arrangement, having considerably more detailed writing, including introductions, transitional and/or modulatory interludes, more than one ensemble chorus, fewer repeated figures, shorter improvised solos, generally more elaborate than 1 and beginning to drift away from small-group idioms.

3. The compositionally oriented arrangement, vastly more specific and detailed than 1 or 2; likely a grand score for larger instrumentation, mixed idioms or styles, leaning toward form, orchestration, and traditional composition, and leaning away from small-group concepts, improvisation, and perhaps the very style the music pretends to be.

Instrumental ranges

Study the ranges for all instruments, memorizing the ones you expect to use most often. Learn the clef and transposition for each, and observe (by listening and noticing) the practical range for each instrument. Each note you write for a specific instrument should be heard in the mind on that instrument as a precaution against writing uncomfortable notes. Find the instrumental ranges on the keyboard to develop a *visual* precaution against writing the uncomfortable or the impossible—you are likely to use a keyboard for working on the details of your arrangements anyway.

Score and parts

There are many ways to organize the paperwork of a score. There are full scores, condensed scores, piano scores, conductor's guides, and no score. Each has its advantages and disadvantages. The full score has everything on it, each instrument with its own staff, but it is difficult to read, if easy to copy. The condensed score or the conductor's guide work well in performance, but are virtually useless in reading, copying, or checking for wrong notes in the copied parts. The piano score is good as a means of reviewing and rereading your scores, and all the notes are there, but the instrument assignments are not, so the piano score is not satisfactory for copying or checking notes. There are transposed scores and concert scores (untransposed). Transposed scores are easy to copy but difficult to reread. Untransposed scores are easy to read, but the copyist has to be mindful of which of several transpositions must be sustained until the part is completely copied. There are many different kinds of score paper, too. What works for some does not necessarily work for others, because we all develop our own score organization. The fundamentals of notation should be learned and practiced to facilitate copying speed and accuracy.

Score reading

Observe the arrangements of others by reading their scores, both with and without piano. Learn how the "collect" is used, as well as other time-saving techniques arrangers use in getting their music on paper—even the techniques that seem to be unique with a particular arranger. Study others' voicings, rhythms, and orchestrational techniques. Consider the overall form or organization of the arrangement.

Chord-scale nomenclature

Study chords of every type, their extensions (9ths, 11ths, 13ths), their function, inversions, voicings, alterations, substitutions, and the accompanying scale for each.

Bibliography

Investigate some of the best books on jazz arranging. David Baker's *Arranging and Composing*[2] is a very thorough study and I highly recommend it. Russell Garcia's *The Professional Arranger-Composer*[3] has been around for nearly twenty years, yet it is still a fine text for arranging. Also recommended are the two books by William Russo, *Composing for the Jazz Orchestra* and *Jazz Composition and Orchestration*,[4] and the Dick Grove method.[5]

SPECIFICS FOR STUDY

The serious student of jazz arranging should involve himself in the following activities and areas of study:

1. Harmony
   a. close voicing
   b. open voicing
   c. spacing (between voices)
   d. voice leading
   e. the unison

[2] Chicago: Maher, 1970.
[3] New York: Criterion Music Publishers, 1954.
[4] Chicago: University of Chicago Press, 1961 and 1968, respectively.
[5] *Guide to Writing Arrangements for Stage Band Ensembles* (Los Angeles: First Place, 1970).

     f. harmonization of nonharmonic tones

     g. harmonization of rhythmic anticipations

2. Melody
   a. revising rhythms of a given melody
   b. motifs and melodic development
   c. creative melody writing

3. Form
   a. formal fragments, such as introductions, solo sections, interludes and transitions, ensemble chorus, codas, backgrounds, special effects, etc.
   b. overall intensity curve as it is affected by orchestration, compositional devices, and the manner of performance
   c. the successful intensity curve

4. Chord progression styles
   a. traditional or standard
   b. be-bop
   c. modern (jazz)
   d. rock-pop
   e. chord substitution principles
   f. cadences-turnarounds (or turnbacks)

5. Compositional devices
   a. melodic-motif development
   b. interval writing
   c. parallelism
   d. polychords and polytonality
   e. pedal point
   f. counterpoint
   g. tension-release principle
   h. stylistic devices

6. Orchestration
   a. bass lines, vamps (ostinato), and bass parts
   b. drum figures and drum parts
   c. keyboard-guitar idioms and vamps
   d. coordinating two keyboards (e.g., piano and guitar)
   e. rhythm section idioms and vamps
   f. unisons
   g. duet and two-part writing (in 3rds, 6ths, 4ths, etc.)

   h. section solis (e.g., saxophone or brass soli)

   i. brass mutings

   j. woodwinds (clarinets, flute, oboe, and bassoon, usually played by saxophonists in jazz bands)

   k. hybridity (mixing of dissimilar instruments, perhaps one or two from each section, often with mutes of more than one kind striving for a unique quality and blend)[6]

   l. extramusical effects for all instruments[7] (e.g., glissandi, doits, growls, feedback, etc.)

   m. use of the concertino group (an implied small group of mixed instruments contrasted with a larger group composed of the remaining players)

Arrangers, like improvisers, develop very personal styles, affected by their training, taste, experience, creative gifts, and personality—musical and otherwise. There are natural leanings in each, too, that may cause one arranger to rely more heavily on his creative melodies, another to rely on orchestrational techniques, another to utilize a known group of performers and draw upon their existing style, and another to rely on exceptionally good musical taste or editorship. Each is a valid concept, as were the prementioned approaches to structuring an arrangement—loose, traditional, and compositional. Our task, as students of arranging, is to learn to appreciate *all* the approaches and techniques used by others. You will, of course, develop a list of favored arrangers, to whom you will listen more often. A partial list of my favorites includes Duke Ellington, Charles Mingus, David Baker, Gil Evans, Ron Miller, Clare Fischer, Quincy Jones, J. J. Johnson, Gunther Schuller, John Carisi,

---

[6] Listen, for example, to the brilliant orchestrations of Gil Evans, who uses hybridity often.

[7] Baker's arranging book, mentioned earlier, contains an excellent listing of extramusical devices for all instruments.

Johnny Mandel, Jeff Sturges, Joe Zawinul, Herbie Hancock, Neal Hefti, Michel Legrand, Oliver Nelson, Klaus Ogerman, Torrie Zito, John Lewis, and Lalo Schifrin. I appreciate other writers for their tune writing alone, though their arrangements are more scarce—people like Chick Corea, Stanley Clarke, Thelonius Monk, Jim Webb, Carole King, Joni Mitchell, Miles Davis, Charles Parker, John Coltrane, George Russell, Horace Silver, Ornette Coleman, Tadd Dameron, Dizzy Gillespie, George Gershwin, Harold Arlen, Wayne Shorter, Billy Strayhorn, plus most of the arrangers listed earlier.

It would be difficult to single out one arranger-songwriter from the foregoing lists as being the best, or one whose talents seem to pervade all areas and techniques of good writing, but certainly one of the best was the late Duke Ellington. He wrote incessantly for about fifty years, creating some of the best songs and jazz lines ever written, in unsurpassed quantity. He was a player of the first rank and understood the performing and improvising musicians for whom he wrote. He never forgot what jazz is; nor did he forget the importance of retaining improvisation and the need to utilize small-group concepts (even in a full-sized band). Duke was more daring than most, even in the earlier years—always trying new ideas, unafraid of the unison texture, stinging dissonances, or jazz intonation. His melodies developed and unfolded like a good symphony, as did the form in general, and a thrilling climax was assured. Ellington wrote pop songs, dance music, concert music, and sacred music. His innovative genius produced new colors in orchestration, and his utilization of the human voice was incorporated in unique ways.

As an influential composer-arranger, Ellington is responsible for many of the details of arrangements done by people who adored him—Charles Mingus, Clare Fischer, Gil Evans, and Gunther Schuller, to mention a few. His most ardent disciple, however, was the amazing Billy Strayhorn, the only other arranger who was accepted by Duke as a co-writer for the great Ellington band. Strayhorn not only arranged well, but he also wrote exceptional tunes, like "Lush Life," "Chelsea Bridge," and even Duke's theme, "Take the 'A' Train." The two musical personalities of Ellington and Strayhorn merged so well that most musicians, even those most strongly influenced by them, have difficulty remembering which tunes and/or arrangements were written by Duke and which by Billy. It may be a long, long time before another writer of comparable individual magnitude appears, much less a perfect and fruitful alliance of two musical giants.

AFTERWORD

To become a well-rounded jazz musician will take time and patience. I don't recall anyone who has accomplished such a goal in less than two or three years, and I would guess that the norm is more like five years—or longer. When you stop to think that the average course in jazz at some institution of higher learning lasts four months, perhaps eight months for a two-semester course, it becomes obvious that we are exposed, intellectually, to many theoretical materials which cannot be fully assimilated at the time of presentation. Months and years will pass, perhaps, before such theoretical ideas are ready to be heard and played to satisfaction. Similarly, this book can be read in a relatively short time, yet it may be years before each of the ideas contained has been learned to the point that its usefulness is fully realized. For those who have difficulty organizing their practice habits, the time lag between presentation and fruition can be especially frustrating. To them I would like to offer some advice. Very few people use their time to maximum efficiency. Minutes and hours of time pass unnoticed by most of us every day. Learn to use those minutes and hours, rather than wait for a longer, "more reasonable" time later. If there isn't time to do *everything*, then do *something*. It is better to concentrate on a smaller number of items, anyway, than to attempt everything in one session. If you laid five bricks a day, at the end of the year you'd have a 10′ x 10′ practice room. If you copied one part from a score each day (taking about twenty minutes), by the end of a year you'd have copied twenty-four arrangements for a fifteen-piece band. If you drive to school or work, put a tape player in your auto. If the trip is only twenty minutes each way, and you stay at home on evenings and weekends, you can still listen to about 165 hours of music (or 230 LPs) in a year. An average pattern for improvisation can be learned in about half an hour. If you practice a new pattern each day, in a year's time you'd have 365 patterns—more than the number (324) found in *Patterns for Jazz*.[1] By following all these suggestions, at the end of the year you'd have a brick practice room, twenty-four arrangements copied (which also can bring in #250–#500), listened to 230 LPs, and gained 365 patterns! The foregoing illustrations may not coincide with your goals or the time span in which you hope to accomplish your goals, but whatever your goals and time availability, it should be obvious to you that without forsaking many, if any, of your present activities, you can become what you wish to be.

[1] Coker, op. cit.